Think I'll Go Eat a Worm

Essays

Amy Wright

Iris Press Chapbook Series
Oak Ridge, Tennessee

ISBN: 978-1-60454-509-8

Cover Photograph: "Hoopoe" by Bruno Mathieu

Illustrations: Kell Alexander Black

Acknowledgments

Kenyon Review: "Mēl"
McSweeney's Internet Tendency: "번데기 (*Beondegi* canned)"
Passages North Online: "Mǣl"
Written River: "Melu"
Waveform: Anthology of Women Essayists (University of Georgia Press): "THIHACOIAAGT"
Gastronomica: The Journal of Critical Food Studies: "Think I'll Go Eat a Worm"

Book Design: Robert B. Cumming, Jr.

Iris Publishing Group, Inc
www.irisbooks.com

Contents

Mēl

When I was ten, I mixed a two-quart bottle of milk in the kitchen sink every morning from powder and hot water and carried it on the back of a four-wheeler to a Black Angus calf I named Michael. The dairy powder would clump at the bottom of the jug like baking soda in a brownie, and I would break it apart with a long-handled spoon my mother reserved for this task.

The milk didn't smell or look like the creamy jug we had in our refrigerator, but like the Life-cereal kid, Mikey always liked it. He would suckle the rubber teat with frothing mouth, filling his belly with guzzles that came faster than nursing. When the bottle was drained, I offered a finger and patted his soft jawline. He would slurp the faux nipple slimy into the ridged roof of his mouth as if it, too, might yield something. Mikey would have drunk another bottle if I had it. If cows don't butt their calves away, they will suckle long after they are yearlings.

• • •

Meal (mēl) *n.* The quantity of milk given by a cow at any one milking; also, the time of milking, e.g., *R. W. Dickson Practical Agriculture* (1807): it may be fitted up with such coolers as are sufficient to contain a meal's milk.

• • •

The world when my baby-boomer mother was born in 1950 contained two and a half billion people. By the time she reached fifty that number more than doubled to pass six billion. Currently over seven billion, the global populace is slated to reach nine or ten billion by 2050. If my access to nutrition, water, and needed medicines remains the same, I can expect to be among the mouths counted.

The green cleaning supplies brand Seventh Generation would have us look to the future we are leaving to distant progeny with our purchases, but my grandfather was the fifth-generation owner of a Virginia Century Farm. Counting from him, I *am* the seventh generation, and the choices being left to an abstract future are fast redounding to me.

During my grandfather's days of animal husbandry, one could watch the balance tipping between arable land, its tenders, and a manageable herd of animals. His generation was already producing more livestock than his parents and grandparents combined, who predominantly planted and maintained apple orchards, kept only a few hens for eggs and cows for milk to barter. He installed equipment to machine-milk the herd but refused to supplement with hormones to increase their production.

He bought and renovated rental houses to supplement the dairy income. My grandmother got a job at the nylons factory, rifled flea-market bins for bargains, while other farms incorporated to meet the large-scale feed demands for livestock.

When my mother and her relatives inherited the farm, they found themselves among a diminishing number of small-scale operators. Facing the decision to sell, my parents chose to make the sacrifices necessary to keep the land, tend their livestock. They wake in the pre-dawn hours before their full-time jobs begin and pull a third shift in the evening after work, often farming by tractor light.

When visiting, I sometimes wake to find headlights combing the starry field beside their house, like low moons orbiting another planet.

• • •

Milky Way *n.* a broad, faintly luminous band seen across the sky at night, consisting of distant stars and nebulae; the galaxy.

• • •

Twelve thousand years ago, bands of neolithic humans took the single most affecting step yet to accommodate a denser population planet. Leaving behind the epipaleolithic earth of a hunter-gatherer lifestyle, they began setting up camps in an agrarian world. The Neolithic Revolution signified a shift in human evolution that combined the cultivation of wild plants, which may have begun as many as six thousand years earlier, with the domestication of animals. These paired technologies, known as the invention of agriculture, enabled them to sustain more people per square foot than foraging and hunting alone, though whether this innovation was demand-induced or supply-led is open for debate. What is known is their rising numbers corresponded to an increasing ability to support themselves.

The most profound aspect of this stride forward, according to archeologist Frank Hole, is the "shift from an immediate to a delayed return system, with its attendant changes in the dependence of one person on another." This social and psychological ability to delay gratification, collaborate, and settle in one place enabled many other changes to come about, including trade economies, nonportable art, writing, and the foundation of those villages it purportedly takes to raise a child, let alone maintain a flock of goats.

Archeobotanist Marijki van der Veen posits that while a flash of genius and desire for change are necessary components, *need* for change in the form of population growth was likely the dominant incentive in the Agricultural Revolution.

•   •   •

According to the Feasting model, proposed by archeologist Brian Hayden, agricultural development and the corresponding evolution of farm implements may have been driven by the desire to exert political dominance and display power by giving feasts. Learning this theory, I picture the Communist ensign of the sickle, symbol of the peasants, under the long shadow of tables at which someone stands head.

•   •   •

The image of abundance conjured by the phrase "milk and honey" recurs in several passages in the Bible, including Exodus 3:8, in which the Lord encourages Moses to lead the Israelites out of Egypt, saying "I have come down…to bring them up out of that land and to a good and broad land flowing with milk and honey."

•   •   •

The United States is the largest single-country agricultural exporter in the world, followed by the Netherlands.

•   •   •

Current food production will need to almost double to meet the demands of the rising global population, though an 1877 telegram published by *The New York Times* reports that all but 1 percent of the nation's arable land "has already been taken up."

•   •   •

The May 2013 United Nations report on "Future Prospects for Food and Feed Security" offers some solutions to the predictable crisis in conventional farming practices. In order to meet the livestock demand of a rising global population whose progress is increasingly accompanied by meat consumption, we must reconsider the dominant animal markets.

Those inefficient converters of feed, the Food and Agriculture Organization suggests, could be profitably augmented by the cultivation of insect species for livestock and aquaculture feed, as well as human consumption. For instance, edible cricket species such as *Acheta domesticus* and *Gryllus bimaculatus* require twelve times less feed than cattle and six times less than pigs to produce the same amount of protein.

•   •   •

Pat Crowley was a river guide in the Grand Canyon when he learned the Colorado River, drained along its route for irrigation, no longer reaches the ocean. In an effort to conserve freshwater, he founded a company called Chapul that makes protein energy bars without soy or dairy but with cricket flour, dates, nuts, and chocolate.

Talking to an ABC News reporter about the psychological obstacle for some Americans to eating insects, Crowley says he researched how other industries have overcome similar cultural barriers. He found that sushi was deemed "repulsive" before it became acclimated to the mainstream, so he seeks to introduce crickets into the American diet with such standard bearers as peanut butter and chocolate the way sushi chefs rolled mango, cucumbers, and rice around small chunks of raw salmon to transition the new taste and texture.

•　•　•

Mēl *n.* Gothic for time, hour.

Time *n.* A limited period or interval, as between two successive events: from base *day* "to cut up or divide." See *tide:* Old English *tīd v.* to surmount (a difficulty, obstacle, etc.); or to "turn the tide," by reversing the course of events.

•　•　•

Oil pops on my first date with Don as he pours Albariño into the hot skillet. I stir the risotto, looking over my shoulder while he pinches grains from the salt pig on the counter and grinds pepper onto the two dozen sautéing crickets. "I should have bought more," I say, admitting it wasn't two standard meat servings I was considering with my purchase. "They were scuttling in the bag beneath my fingers, and I wasn't sure I could do it."

"You don't have to," he says, even as they are turning a toasty chestnut color before us.

"I think I can eat them now that they're cooked. It was entombing them in the freezer that gave me pause. It's so much easier to buy shrimp," I say, familiar with deveining shrimp, pulling off their pink legs.

Unsure how to prepare these land prawns before serving them, I invited him, an entomologist at the university where we both teach, to dinner. There are insect cookbooks available in

English, including recipes for Cricket Croquettes and Crickets a la Papouasie, but Peter Menzel, coauthor with his wife Faith D'Aluisio of *Man Eating Bugs*, recommends one eats insects for the first time with someone who has done it before—unless she has access to a restaurant where they are on the menu. I imagine an upscale Nashville restaurant makes *chapulines* available the way Guelaguetza, L.A.'s premier Oaxacan restaurant does—as an off-menu item—but I want to taste them with minimal augmentation to get a true sense of their flavor.

Don reassures me that while grasshopper legs can get stuck in your teeth and should be removed, crickets can keep their appendages, which soften like the petiole of a spinach leaf.

•　•　•

We have lost familiarity with the way our ancestors survived, Menzel says. In comparison to wild game, insects were a convenience food. "Grab a wooly caterpillar and throw it on the fire and burn off all the urticating hairs," he says, detailing a typical dinner under the stars, "and you've got this protein and it's all cooked."

•　•　•

Meolc *n.* Old English for an opaque white or bluish-white liquid secreted by the mammary glands of female mammals, serving for the nourishment of their young. Not *milt, v.* that which passes, dwindles, or fades gradually.

•　•　•

Insect gathering and rearing at the household or industrial level, proposes Dr. Marcel Dicke, scientist and professor at Waginengen University in the Netherlands and visiting professor at Cornell University, can ameliorate the current rate of deforestation, environmental degradation, greenhouse gas emissions, and contamination of surface water with biological waste.

•　•　•

The intricate machines of these exoskeletons do not break down visually from cooking. They soften but retain their glistening form, their compound eyes, their ovipositors and long, segmented antennae, their wings. They deepen in shade like blackened catfish. "Their back legs have tiny muscles," I notice, looking closely at a leg that has come off in the pan, which I expected to be a bare thread of chitin.

"From all that jumping," Don says, as I lift it to my mouth like a miniature frog leg. The taste is similar, meaning mild and easily dominated by salt and white wine, but the texture is much lighter. It conjures a flake of rainbow trout or butter bean that melts like an ice sliver away from its skin, disappearing faster than a crystal on a sorbet spoon.

"To new adventures!" we toast, clinking glasses over the pan of delicacies.

• • •

The New York Times ran a series of articles on unusual greens, inspired by the health dangers of limiting our palates. One article, titled "Breeding the Nutrition Out of Our Food," explains that plant nutrition began to weaken when we stopped foraging wild breeds. Though we depend on cultivated species, the series promotes and provides recipes for a wider range of varieties such as purslane, beet greens, and amaranth—dark green leafy vegetables, used in a number of world cuisines, that are more often considered weeds and absent from American markets.

Far more nutritious than common species, dandelion greens, for example, have seven times the phytonutrients of spinach, or those compounds whose anti-inflammatory, detoxifying, and antioxidant effects have the potential to "reduce the risk of four of our modern scourges: cancer, cardiovascular disease, diabetes, and dementia." Purslane has more omega-3 fatty acids than any other leafy vegetable, in addition to calcium, potassium, vitamin K, and an impressive amount of vitamin A. Our privileging of certain species, the article makes clear, should be reevaluated in relation to changing criteria and access to information.

• • •

Preliminary studies of insect nutritional composition are promising, but Dicke says much more investigation is needed to determine the most efficient species with the highest proportion of protein, minerals, vitamins, amino acids, and omega-3 and -6 fatty acids.

More studies are also needed because our ability to digest the high fiber in insects appears to increase with dietary exposure. According to an Italian study, the presence of chitinase in human gastric juices after ingesting insects is more prevalent in tropical countries where insects are regularly consumed. Chitinase is the digestive enzyme that breaks down the glycosidic walls in chitin, the main component of insect exoskeletons, much like cellulose in plants.

According to the American Academy of Allergy, Asthma and Immunology: worldwide sensitization rates to one or more common allergens among school children are currently approaching 40–50 percent. Also, of food allergic children, peanut is the most prevalent allergen, followed by milk.

The allergy-hygiene hypothesis suggests that the consumption of insects in early childhood could support better protection against allergies later in life. Drawing upon evidence that allergies are lower in developing countries, the theory proposes that an increase of chitinase in the digestive track contributes to fewer allergic reactions because chitin has been associated with defense against parasitic infections and some allergic conditions.

• • •

After I stir the plump, simmering grains of Arborio rice to a creamy consistency, I arrange the sculptural forms of the crickets on our risotto, where they glisten like truffles. But I am not confident I will be able to consume them the way I am accustomed to downing dressed poultry or rib meat.

• • •

Milk-and-water, *adj.* Lacking will or strength, wishy-washy, namby-pamby.

• • •

That Mikey would be sold for slaughter I knew. That the money would be used to start my first savings account I discovered after he was sold as a steer. Blood money, some might say, but to my mind, that money was a lump-sum allowance, a starter culture for my college fund, an initiation into the grown-up economy. It was about that time I joined the adults in the dining room, graduating from the "kids' table" during family holidays.

• • •

Many vegans and vegetarians achieve complete nutritional balance with diligent food combinations without meat, but it is not possible for everyone for a host of reasons, including food allergies, access to a variety of whole foods, and expense. An ecologically sound, fast-cooking, affordable protein and amino-acid source that can supplement more diets stands to reason against inherited fears.

• • •

Lifting a forkful of cricket mushroom risotto, I eyeball (precisely the right verb) these wide-eyed, if unseeing, creatures. Years of startling at insects condition me to react with alarm, but seeing them stilled, pacific, and out of context with surprise reconditions that automatic response. I examine a cricket's lens the way I once looked at a buckeye fallen from the tree in front of my grandparents' farmhouse. I look long, the way I paused in midstride on a running trail to hold a doe's gaze. I study its ridged tegmen, or modified forewings, the way I examined the back of a bookshelf after my mother taught me to discern cherry wood from mahogany.

In my mouth, the cricket breaks apart like a mushroom cap pearled with rice or an artichoke heart, a corn chip softened by salsa. But it is only akin to these things, being an experience unto itself. I fill with wonder such that I have not experienced since my tongue first encountered another's. The mystery under scrutiny is part of this dish's savor.

· · ·

Professor Dicke is among those contemporary voices urging entomophagy, or the dietary cultivation of insects, as a fast-growing renewable food source. In particular, he advocates a cultural revolution in Europe and America to join the other 80 percent of the world who already make insects part of their diets.

I had the opportunity to meet Dicke at the Netherlands Embassy in Washington, D.C., along with his wife, Alida Maandag, who helped prepare the cicadas I sampled for the first time. They enjoy a plateful or more of the delicacies a week, Dicke says, at least while they are at home, where it is possible to find restaurants and retailers that market breeds reared for human consumption.

Dicke praises variety as a perk of this dietary alternative. With over one thousand species of edible insects, it is possible to extend our menus in hundreds of unforeseen directions.

· · ·

Traditional livestock waste generates 18 percent more CO_2 than automobile transmissions, whereas insects produce relatively few GHGs and very little ammonia. They also need a fraction of the freshwater required by cattle, pigs, and chickens.

· · ·

When he is not being my dining companion or professing to future scientists and farmers, Don manages an organic garden that serves area hungry. For our second dinner date, "Crispy Mealys with Spring Greens"—modified from *The New York Times* series, we forage the unmown margins of the garden for poke, lamb's quarters, dandelion greens, and plantain. My great-grandmother (who lived to ninety-eight) harvested such wild varieties from the woods behind her house to feed seven children during the Great Depression. Considering her logic, I add a few tablespoons of maple syrup to the sauté sauce to counter any remaining bitterness in the greens.

Don boils brown rice and ladles it onto our plates along with the lightly caramelized greens. In a separate pan, we flash-fry mealworms, or darkling beetle larva (*Tenebrio molitor*). These hazel creatures, the size of slivered almonds, crackle in the oil like pork chop edges. Blowing on one pulled hot from the pan, he offers me what tastes like a crisp and airy crouton.

Examining the golden crowns of mealys atop their beds of greens, I tally the network of relationships represented on the table—from the Vermont maple tree-tappers and California rice farmers to the often-unseen forces that pollinate vegetables and flowers, enrich the soil's mineral content, control plant-eating pests, and now provide a low carbohydrate-to-protein ratio. Resplendent with chlorophyll, the greens glow beneath the gilded mealys, shining like the sunlight their leaves absorbed. Instead of pricking my conscience, I appreciate the apparent interrelationships, remembering the words of Quaker Buddhist shepherd Mary Rose O'Reilley, who says it is "a mark of reverence for the animals to take perfect care of their meat and to waste nothing."

• • •

The next day I put in an order for a starter mini-livestock herd of mealworms. Crickets have a higher proportion of protein (at 64.1 percent) and tested superior to soy protein as an amino acid source, but mealys contain omega-3 and -6 fatty acids in the same proportion as fish, the amino acids leucine and lysine sold as supplements in drugstores, and calcium, potassium, magnesium, iron, and zinc similar to beef. Plus, they are reputed to be an easy species to tend.

Not counting the innumerable gnats I've gulped on running trails, the stray black soldier fly ground unseen in my peanut butter, or the bee that stung my esophagus on the way down during a bike ride, my first intentional exoskeletal bite feels like striding into a new world. With it, I left behind the one in which Aldous Huxley says beliefs are determined by poorly reasoned conditioning. The divide loomed large as an entoingénue. Afterward, it was just a line in the sand, a step taken like many others, if over the moon: where the cow jumps, and I lick the would-be runaway spoon.

Think I'll Go Eat A Worm

Nobody likes me, everybody hates me
Think I'll go eat a worm

One of the great takeaways from my preschool was that counterculture anthem, "Think I'll Go Eat A Worm," although I did not mutter it with the down-in-the-mouth self-pity that characterizes The Kids in the Hall's comedy sketch, "Nobody Likes Us." I belted it out with the exuberance of entertaining that almost-unimaginable prospect of downing a live noodle that just might slither to my intestines only to crawl back up! The horror gave me a thrill of courage, a jolt of daring, and I sang the chorus loudly, often, and with pride, to think myself capable of something my parents would *never* try. It was as revolutionary an idea as not taking what other people thought of you too seriously, though I would not appreciate this layer of the song until high school when it came back to me after my physics teacher, Mr. Pope, told us anecdotally that the fastest cooking, lowest energy demanding protein to hunt if lost in the woods is not rabbits and squirrels but earthworms.

EVOLVING THE NORM

Young people's willingness to embrace far-out ideas is what prompts Robert Nathan Allen to reach out to them in the pursuit of more sustainable livestock industries. Founder of Little Herds, Inc., a nonprofit based in Austin, Texas, Allen leads adventurous workshops for the generations who will be making the hard decisions about how to feed the nine or ten billion mouths expected by 2050. Gathered around this blonde bearded character, these groups of children do more than sing about eating worms. They chomp them in finger Jell-O and oatmeal raisin cookies, their afternoon snacks enhanced with protein, B vitamins, and omega-3 fatty acids. Plus, they get to wow their parents, waiting in the wings, by trying things they often never have.

Less conditioned by existing standards, young Americans are not as inhibited by the fears of their parents, who are often reached while looking over their children's shoulders, Allen says. Therefore, he creates opportunities at area parks, community centers, and art galleries to capitalize on youths' fearlessness toward new experiences.

In addition to attending these bug festivals and zipping out smart phones to click on info-graphics he provides, I picture his audience traveling to Cameroon, Mexico City, and Tokyo, bringing stories from travels farther and farther abroad back to middle school classrooms. The increasing access and exposure of each generation to the rest of the world motivates greater understanding and consideration of a wider network of consumers and producers, and could close the divide between westerners and those who already enjoy eating insects.

In some cases, travel has already acquainted children or their parents with chitinous delicacies. Spicy fried crickets, water beetles, and bamboo worms are sold by Thai vendors, and Mexican *chapulines,* or grasshoppers, make delicious tacos enjoyed since the ancient Aztecs toasted them with garlic, salt, and lime juice. Like one's inaugural international flight, that first bite changes everything, and in my experience, it only takes one ento-enhanced meal to make the psychological transition. Before I sampled my first mealy, I couldn't have imagined making them part of my diet the way Namibians do when mopane worms are in season, roasting the meaty marshmallows in hot ashes. Afterwards, I could. The power of that shift inspires Allen to direct his energies toward the young and ready members of this growing movement.

WORM IS A MISNOMER

Mealworms are not worms at all, but the juvenile form of darkling beetles before they undergo metamorphosis. Nor does the comparison to those thankless aerators of the soil do them justice, since they are not damp and squishy, but dry and smooth as pumpkin seeds. Plus, when reared for human consumption, they need never touch mandible to dirt from their golden beds of cornmeal.

When I was a girl trilling, "Down goes the first one," I imagined the slimy nightcrawlers my brother used to fish. Mealys, however, are the size of an almond sliver and coated in a berry-brown shell with the thickness of a popped popcorn kernel. Spooning them roasted onto tortilla chips with salsa and guacamole adds extra crunch to the snack food as well as essential linoleic acids (in quantities higher than beef), iron, potassium, selenium, and zinc. Added to gluten-free bread, mealy flour could provide an alternative for the increasing number of allergen-sensitive people looking for nutritionally complete options to balance their diets.

If concepts about "nobody" liking us, and "everybody" hating us are universal, the fear I had of insect cuisine is not. In fact, insects have supplemented human diets for millennia. In *Edible Insects and Human Evolution,* anthropologist Julie Lesnik details examples of insect foraging in hunter-gather cultures worldwide, including Native American. I've not tried it yet but a friend's cookbook, *American Indian Cooking and Herb Lore,* has a recipe for the delicacy, Yellow-Jacket Soup. Though yellow jackets are wasps rather than bees, the dish recalls my other favorite childhood song, "I'm Bringing Home A Baby Bumblebee," and in fact, protein-rich bee larvae are eaten by Chinese for their medicinal properties and are savored by gourmands for more than their stores of zinc, riboflavin, copper, and iron.

WHY NOT EAT INSECTS?

But why would anyone nosh worms when there are hamburgers available? One reason, Allen makes clear in his kid-friendly talks, is that insects convert grain to protein at an approximately 1:1 ratio of conversion, as opposed to the 10:1 ratio of cattle. They also generate a fraction of the greenhouse gases emitted by traditional livestock, and require much less fresh water to produce. One pound of insect flour saves approximately 500 gallons of H_2O compared to one pound of beef. Plus, with over 900 edible species, insects offer opportunities to expand our menus with tantalizing new options.

But Allen also makes clear that children should no more start chomping bugs they find in their backyard than they would take a bite out of a cow in a field or a fish in a local pond. World Entomophagy, the supplier that provides the insects he samples, operates according to strict regulations for human consumption.

What encourages me, heir to woeful worm-eating lyrics, is that Allen sees this new menu option as an exciting opportunity. While insects have been eaten for thousands of years, they have never been domesticated and cultivated. They have been mostly seasonally harvested, as in the case of mopane worms, or, like silkworm pupae, a byproduct of another process. Considering that even classic foods like apples have long been bred selectively to achieve their sweet snap, domestication could significantly improve insects' nutritional and economic value and zest. Plus, with over 900 edible insect varieties, they provide many new taste sensations to explore.

Bruschetta with a Side of Adrenalin

Though I had already sampled mealys and crickets prior to meeting Allen, I was looking forward to trying cicadas for the first time, even as imagining it gave me a thrill of nervous energy. My brother's friends, owners of Suzuki GSXs and red Camaros, would not consider me a daredevil on a bike, but even those brazen young men hesitate before popping a tried-and-tested gourmet insect into their mouths.

Having seen abandoned molts clinging to trees, I was surprised to find that cooked cicadas were smaller than I expected. These mettle-testers look no more threatening on toasted slices of French bread than a head of asparagus. Still, they are eaten whole as oysters—a swallowing feat I have yet to master. Unlike those amorphous sea creatures, cicadas have distinctive features, including wide-spaced, unblinking eyeballs that gleam back at your omnivorous conscience.

When I bite into the head, its texture is similar to the give of an olive and melts into the drizzle of oil and tomatoes. Basil dominates any pure cicada flavor, so I try a skewered barbequed one on another plate. Like tofu or seitan, cicadas overpower easily by cooking spices, but unlike those foods, these exotic creatures offer diners a rare encounter. Through them, one might come face to face not with that piecemeal picture presented in a flank steak or side of breast meat but with the whole paradigm of one being's dependence on another.

My fellow insect samplers that surround me take our cues from each other when the wait staff brings out another round of laden trays. The bodies of these insects are on display in this feast like nude rose petals in a still life. Though no more seeing than a boiled lobster's, tiny eyes peer back from fingers holding them up on toothpicks. The muscles behind my ears twitch like the foregone antennae Mr. Moore raised years ago, and I ask one young woman who has not yet sampled one: "Are you going to do it?" She nods her head, her dark hair pulled back in a ponytail, and pops a cricket croquette into her mouth.

"What do you think?" I ask. "Yum!" she says. We smile at each other, a little giddy from defying our initial fears, appreciating that we are now joined together on the other side of a seeming gulf, our perspectives altered. I think she likes me. In fact, *everyone* seems to in this roomful of people invested in our collective future. Maybe even loves. Think I'll go eat a worm.

번데기 (*Beondegi*, canned)

Silkworm pupae are not a new food in Asia. Considering the Silk Road winds back to a legend in the 27th century BC that the fourteen-year-old empress Leizu unwound a spool of thread from a cocoon fallen into her teacup, both trade and snack may have emerged simultaneously and scented with jasmine. But I was raised on the milk of Holsteins and the beef of Black Angus, so this red and yellow can covered in Hangul script was new to me.

Beondegi, boiled or steamed and seasoned, are widely available from South Korean street vendors, but fresh delicacies in Nashville are as hard to come by as a record deal. The clerks in the Asian and International Markets shook their heads when my intrepid dining companion, Don, and I asked for them. In one case, they led us to the bait and tackle section of the store.

But we persevered.

Unafraid of cultural bifurcations wherein "me" becomes "you" and something I scrunch my nose at, I offered my best shy southern smile-turned-bodhisattva to the man behind the pungent counter where slabs of fresh eel were laid out like the steaks I was raised on. Over their dead bodies, Don and I asked if they sold any insects, the corners of my mouth upturned as if to say, "Friend, in every measurable way we are different, but let not that divide our mutual love of arthropods. Where do you keep the goods?"

Nothing. You'd think we were asking him for MoonPies, which I saw in hot pink version by the door. We were on our own, white-skinned minorities in an alien land trying to fit in.

A can, tucked between the lemongrasses and pepper pastes, bore a picture of what looked like glistening, if greyish, headless beetles. I was thrilled. Having already eaten crickets, mealworms, wax moth larvae, and cicadas, I looked forward to trying another species of amino acid-rich protein.

My foray into the world of entomophagy, or the human consumption of insects, was prompted by the need to conserve the fresh waterways being siphoned for corporate agriculture. I asked Don, the entomologist at our local university, if he would consent to an interview. Thanks to us both being single, and the uncommonly good cricket mushroom risotto we prepared the following evening, a relationship was born on the wings of forward-thinking culinary ventures. Our own sustainability, though, would be tested when he cracked open this odiferous can.

I will not claim silkworm pupae are themselves unpalatable any more than I would deem all pork inedible based on scrapple, but I will say what tasted like bite-sized turkey livers steeped in formaldehyde did not lend easy romance to our stir fry.

"Maybe fresh with onions and butter," I said, chewing thoughtfully.

"No." He said, "There is no disguising this flavor." His green eyes lost their luster. Fortunately, he recovered his wits and plucked some mint leaves from his herb garden to cleanse our palates. He also had the foresight to buy chocolate coconut-milk ice cream, which he spooned into pale turquoise dishes and carried to the patio where a breeze could rinse the acrid smell from our noses.

"I bought *two* cans!" He remembered, but he didn't threaten our fledgling courtship with a repeat attempt. He fed them to the chickens. The birds scarf up insects quicker than any grain you feed them, but even they nosed them in the dirt as if to let it soak up the soup of monosodium glutamate that preserved them. Apparently, human cultures have more in common than we think, since we can all over-process, or as my grandmother would say "cook to death," anything.

THIHACOIAAGT

A mealworm farm is as quiet as the fall of grain onto grain, like hair. Even mealtime potato noshing is as hushed as a drinking peace lily. They undulate in their oat-bin barn like wind through alfalfa, curl in the corners like miniature golden pepperoni. I purchased my first clew of mealys to answer the increasing need for eco-efficient protein and to continue my family's seven-generation farming heritage. Cove Creek Farm has seen apple orchards rise and fall, clover fields churned to butter, turkey eggs laid and gathered. Great-great-great-great-great grandparents whisper in my ear ways to keep the farm going.

Initially, I offered my mini-livestock to a friend who raises chickens. The hens expressed their preference for this instinctual favorite protein by rushing in ecstatic stampede to pluck the ground clean. Their sunnier yolks made apparent the mineral boost mealworms provide of magnesium, zinc, iron, copper, and manganese, but their high proportion of omega-3 and -6 fatty acids inspired me to add them directly, sautéed, to my plate.

• • •

One of the ten marvels created on the twilight of the earth's first Sabbath, the *shamir,* a small barley-size worm, was used by Moses to engrave the twelve tribes of Israel on the High Priest's breastplate. Later, Solomon employed this supernatural creature to construct the First Temple by outlining every quarry stone needed and placing the worm on these lines. As the shamir crawled along, the stones split asunder without noise, "so that there was neither hammer nor ax nor any tool of iron heard in the house while it was building" (I Kings 6: 7).

• • •

Though not Jewish, I appreciate the dream geneticist Paul Goldstein describes "of all Jews to assist in building the Third (and final) Temple" on a metaphorical level because, like the First Temple built by King Solomon at Jerusalem, it makes Earth a fit dwelling place for God. The very name has been bloodied like the land under the Temple Mount, but the aspiration—to honor The Highest Ideal Humans Are Capable of Imagining at Any Given Time—remains worthwhile. Plus, its acronym, THIHACOIAAGT, is as unpronounceable as the Old Testament *YHWH*.

The Spirit That Moves through All Things, as one friend translates the Cherokee word *Unahlahnauhi,* might be a better term; or prana, as yogis refer to life force; or the Chinese *qì,* for the flow of energy that animates matter. All delineate more clearly an eternal constant than my THIHACOIAAGT, which evolves or devolves in relation to human consciousness. The limitation of this misnomer, though, has its advantage, since the transformation of human behavior can attest to evolutionary development subtler than skeletal structure or cranial mass.

* * *

In this era the highest ideal might be consideration for others—given that the planet supports billions of species and over seven billion humans—or gratitude for the many symbiotic relationships that make this planet habitable. Consider the ten quintillion insects that outnumber all other animals on this planet combined. Often unseen, they contribute to soil fertility, crop production, plant pollination, waste decomposition, pest control, and biodiversity. One could say that insects, in their multitudes, comprise a scaffolding from the lower to higher realms, a pillar that supports earthly life, an invisible axis around which thirty-some phyla spiral in a millimeter-by-kilometer rise.

* * *

The original axis mundi in ancient cosmogonies was a tree, and various cultures and religions reflect that influence. In Scandinavian culture the universe flowered from the boughs of the Yggdrasil Ash, known as the Tree of Existence. The Bodhi tree Buddha meditated beneath illumined reality so purely he too came to mirror it. Hindus drink tea suffused with the divinity of

Vishnu and his wife, Laksmi, inherent in the leaves of the holy basil. The Cheremiss tribe that once existed in Russia protected at all costs their sacred groves from damage or interference. "A clump of trees made a great impression," John Stewart Collis reminds us. "Sometimes they were supposed to be the abode of gods, and sometimes they were regarded simply as natural temples in which gods might be approached."

• • •

In *The Triumph of the Tree,* Collis muses that modern movement away from organized religion might indicate growing direct intimation of the divine. We may be ready to repair our state of being torn from a distant creator, nature, and one another, he says, through realization of "at-one-ment." This underlying sense of unity could take precedence over varying theistic and nontheistic ideologies, he suggests. Beneath dogmas and dermis, blood and bone, nearer even than thought, we stem from the same substance. "We sprang from the oak," Czeslaw Milosz writes. We too send roots into "the dark womb of the earth."

• • •

When I was growing up, our backyard hickory was tall enough that when the occasional nut dropped on our roof, it sounded with a sharp popgun blast. I imagined scenes unfolding in its wide-armed branches—a waifish grandmother braiding her granddaughter's hair, a straw-hatted farmer slicing cherry tomatoes—dreamscapes, since an adjacent ham hock would be wolfing mud pies, a tennis racket batting a giraffe's spine. The branches swayed and shuddered, contrasting each leaf with shadow's edge. When I lay daydreaming on my bed, "trees made conceptual thought possible," as Collis asserts.

Thinking of that green imaginative stimulus, I can picture early humans leaping from their grasp of surrounding baobabs to comprehend the unseen support system bolstering such structures. But water's movement, bird's-eye views, and leafcutter ants' collaborative societies too have contributed to our brain's development. The key to appreciate is that we depend on the natural world directly and indirectly. How could we forget, when the arterial outspread feeding our gray matter resembles a *mopane* tree, named for the Shona word for butterfly?

• • •

"Until people start feeling a connection between their own body and mind and the rest of 'nature,'" David Hinton says, "until they come to understand this as a continuum—they're not going to care" about protecting nature or humanity as a whole. A translator of ancient Chinese verse, Hinton has spent his life studying the deep ecology of poets in the rivers-and-mountains tradition. His work has led him to the same insights he finds in the poetry—that our thought-generated sense of separation is illusory.

• • •

The hickory was already mature when I began studying it, but history was writ large in its anatomy. I flashed my first poetic license noticing a fork spread from its base, like parents, from which emerged two limbs strong enough to support a swing apiece for my brother and me. Its canopy stretched as wide as the family history my Aunt Alpha was tracing. An early illustration of time's processes, decaying limbs had to be trimmed to protect our house, but green shoots flowered in their place. Under the crown, branches thickened and parted, but at the base a burl merged what never had been separate.

• • •

I live in one of the eight states whose percentage for food insecurity, ranging from 16 to 21 percent, is higher than the national 14 percent and global 12 percent averages. How—I ask myself and my neighbors—have we so poorly managed our needs? "It could only have happened," Wendell Berry says, "through our failure to care enough for the world to be humble enough before it, to think competently enough of its welfare." Potential not only for a nation but also this planet to provide enough for everyone without exhausting natural resources is achievable with conscientious cultivation. Is such an ideal not worth our highest regard? The word "worth" shares a root, *weorð,* with "worship," that intimidating noun that would exact excellence.

• • •

Solomon strove to build a permanent dwelling for God to reside among humankind, but in our century, we have seen the conflict that arises when such an ideal is confined to a particular land or sect. Fixtures fall. Ownership is disputed. Our species might better attain its greatest heights the way forests do, by drawing on a more integrative foundation. One cannot point at, only toward, such undergirding. The temple lasts longest made not of marble or bone but of the most estimable action possible at any given moment.

• • •

Our national debt doesn't account for dung beetles, mayflies, honeybees, and thousands of other species that carry our food's chains. In exchange for their mutually beneficial services, we invent stronger pesticides, level forests, pollute waterways, and otherwise attempt to dominate our interdependent environment. But guilt will only daunt our power to act. Nor will we undertake responsibility we cannot manage, and nothing could bolster this charge but the kind of infrastructure that flexes in strong wind, draws on a fundamental substratum, and parses nothing unless it passes through the heartwood.

• • •

The past's failure to create a favorable present or to sustain a viable future prompted Berry to declare the need for "new speech—a speech that will cause the world to live and thrive in men's minds." It takes poetry as its inspiration, since metaphors connect humans to the world around them. Such dialogue would also reaffirm our participation in the ongoing process of creation, through which we might meet or remember spontaneous adoration and from that effusion of feeling make the kind of voluntary emendations that fulfill human promise.

Only a poet could conceive such possibility—perhaps a mad farmer, and the two billion entomophagists already eating insects worldwide.

• • •

Subtitled *The Last Great Hope to Save the Planet,* Daniella Martin's *Edible* makes a case for entomophagy, or the human consumption of insects, to complement the livestock industries working to feed our densely populated planet. Though many contemporary westerners and Europeans startle at the suggestion, Martin appreciates the squeamishness that accompanies those knee-jerk reactions. Overcoming fear can maximize culinary adventure. In an age when familiar packaged and packaged-to-seem-new foods predominate, supplementing our daily rotations with edible insects might rouse the palate and awaken the tongue.

• • •

I have eaten mealworms baked on pizza, folded in tacos, mixed in cornbread, browned in oatmeal cookies, dropped in egg-drop soup, rolled into spaghetti meatballs, and stirred sautéed into tuna salad, which added crunch akin to when I layered my third-grade sandwiches with potato chips. As efficient as they are versatile, mealworms convert grain to protein at the rate of one gram per gram, minimizing agricultural land and water use.

• • •

To silence the many arguments against lofty dreams with actionable means, one must rise high as a bird in flight. In European folklore several birds are granted the power to sever obstacles from some path. Such "opener" birds include the raven, the eagle, the bee-eater, the woodpecker, and the ostrich, among others, but by far the most important is the hoopoe, who holds the famous *shamir.*

"If we go down into ourselves, we find that we possess exactly what we desire," Ewa Chrusciel writes in her book of poems, *Contraband of Hoopoe.* We carry our progeny on our cuffs, circulate inherited breath, and wear ancestral hopes in sheets of finest dust, shed cells skittering toward the earth when we drag our feet.

• • •

While it may seem contradictory to gratitude to cultivate another creature for protein, conscientious animal husbandry has deepened my admiration for other species and my awareness of reliance on them. My generation, though, has tipped the balance for raising enough traditional livestock in comfortable and growth-patient conditions.

• • •

One January I helped my father pull a larger-than-average calf from its first-time mother. After laboring for hours while Dad looked on with binoculars, the cow was exhausted before the head breached. "Once the nostrils make their appearance," he told me, "the calf has separated from the birth canal and relies on the oxygen it can get on its own." When the tired mother retracted the head into her womb, we drove toward them in the vehicle he uses to feed. The familiar engine didn't startle her, but cows separate themselves from the herd to give birth and Number 14 didn't want to be disturbed. Still, we were able to steer her toward a head gate to do what we could.

Dad slipped a finger-width chain around what would be the wrist joint on the calf's hoof to give us purchase to pull. Over the years he has experimented with other devices, but this technique for hand pulling has proven gentlest on the cow's hips. Like many jobs on the farm, it also requires strength. My boots threatened to slip on the manure-slick barn floor, but I dug in my heels and relied on friction from my gloves. "We'll need to protect the calf from falling on the concrete," Dad said, better assuming its odds for survival than I.

Before this calf, I had helped pull two, neither of which lived. Seeing the calf's tongue lolling from its mouth, I thought we were trying to save the young mother's life. Then the calf emerged, ribs expanding with ours while we rushed to prevent its spill.

In our exuberance, we named the calf Lucky. Lucky was lucky she made her appearance on a weekend. Dad has a full-time job to compensate for the vicissitudes of small-time farming. My grandfather could wait for late winter dawns, but Dad feeds before the sun comes up, and by the time he gets home from work, the fields are dark. Sun and stars both shined on Lucky. Born a heifer on a small farm, assuming good health, she will live the full duration of her natural life, birthing calves in natural reproductive cycles, eating hay and grass from spacious pasture without ever seeing a feedlot, and dying of old age.

•   •   •

Michael Pollan in *The Botany of Desire* explains the compulsion of apples, potatoes, tulips, and marijuana to cast their seeds over the widest land possible. He elaborates how their needs drive human appetite as much as humans domesticate them. Applying the same concept to biology equally bends the mind. Like the kingdom *Plantae,* the kingdom *Animalia* strives to propagate foremost and diversely. Outside my parents' kitchen window, Lucky kicks up her hooves and dashes across the hillside, every cell bursting with Black Angus genetics.

•   •   •

Meanwhile, somewhere under a flour drift, the world's crispiest mealworm is strategizing ways to carry on.

•   •   •

After centuries of use and adoption by cultures around the world, a recent increase in insect diets by westerners and

Europeans are prompting more research into mini-livestock's nutritional and ecological advantages. Scientists are learning which species provide the most health benefits, rear easily, best augment existing livestock industries as feed, and thrive on food-industry byproducts like apple juice pulp, melon rinds, and carrot skins.

A Polish university study found the most nutritious way to serve mealworms appears to be milling them into flour. As flour, mealworms yield twice the protein, fat, and mineral content as fresh. The high-quality meal this team studied was created by boiling larvae, as one might shrimp, for three minutes, and then drying them at sixty degrees Celsius. This form of processing has the added advantage of convenience. Enriching bread or protein bars with mealworm flour takes less time than it takes to unwrap a package of ground beef.

• • •

Some have suggested, like beef and pork, mealworms need a name that distinguishes them as foodstuffs rather than creatures. Author Joanne Greenberg suggests the term "shamir," after the thought-to-be-vanished, heaven-sent creature.

Shamir tacos might stimulate more appetites on restaurant menus. Shamir burgers could pick up where ostrich burgers left off—their lean meat equally free of saturated fat but easier to tend. I particularly want to see shamir flour listed as an ingredient, because the English translation of mealworms' Latin name, *Tenebrio molitor,* stems from the root verb *molitus,* meaning to build or construct, to labor at, and to set in motion, with the suffix suggesting one who builds, constructs, mills.

• • •

My uncle H.A. inherited Reed Creek Milling Company from his father after years hefting infant-size sacks of corn meal to stock local groceries. Until I visited when I was nine, I pictured a wooden wheel, as in our painting of Mabry Mill, churning the creek into frothy purls of mist. In reality, a sheath hides the wheel's action while grist stacks like snow clouds spilling powdery flakes. The heady smell of sweet grain fills the air, which one can just distinguish from grass cud, the sough of milled wheat from snuffling cattle.

It is not impossible to imagine a peanut-size creature carving its way onto the production line. Nor does it seem a reach to call such a solution miraculous, considering it could well-provision homes for the next highest human cause, befitting Solomon's goal, without the instruments of war.

Mæl

Mæl n. from the Old English for measure, fixed time.

•   •   •

A cubed Hanover Better Boy drizzles its citrus broth into a pudding of avocado. Bell peppers wait in the chopper to be added to a dish of jalapeño pentacles. Crunchy flakes of salt, a shock of lime wedges, purple onions are laid out in mango-colored bowls to provide bite to the accruing party-size vat of guacamole. The chip option, white corn. A pan on the counter cools the final topper—two pounds of mealys, their golden bodies fried crisp, the size of American Girl Doll fingers.

As the larval phase of darkling beetles, yellow mealworms do not feel much like worms. Unlike the larvae of wax-moths, which have the texture of custard with a day-old skin, mealworms are slick as dried beans.

•   •   •

The chef, Daniella Martin, founder of GirlMeetsBug.com, says the strength of Americans' resistance to entomophagy, or the human consumption of insects, can be used to change their minds. "To have an aversion so deep it's become visceral," she says, "really gets people to pay attention to your message with their whole bodies."

Martin and I, along with a crowd of reporters, foodies, area professors, scientists, and entomologists are in The Netherlands Embassy in Washington, D.C. A staff member confirmed my name on the press list and welcomed me with a gift, a white box I later open to find a computer mouse partially filled with blue liquid in which floats a cheese wedge, a cow the same size as the miniature hen, tomato, and carrot. Its label, Holland Food Partner. A sunshine-orange banner on the wall of the conference room explains: "Holland is second only to the United States in agricultural export."

On a neighboring banner, handsome families flash hominy-white smiles above a collage of green beans, fronds of spinach, ears of corn gleaming like my dairy-farming cousin Al's blonde locks on posters for our high school agriculture organization. Though insects are available for purchase in grocery stores in The Netherlands, they are not yet displayed in this bounty.

• • •

The nutrition crisis is not yet visible in all parts of the world, but what is apparent is the spreading popularity of western dietary habits. The 44 lbs. of animal protein averaged annually in developing nations is growing to equal the European 120 kg (166 lbs.) and American 265 lbs. The population increase marks an unsustainable consumption of our planet's resources if more efficient converters of protein are not used to augment the dominant livestock markets of pigs and cattle.

• • •

The Goshute Indians of Utah, accustomed to eating grasshoppers, locusts, and crickets, christened shrimp "sea crickets" upon first sampling them.

Eating stir fry the day after mushroom cricket risotto, shrimp feels bulbous in my mouth, fatty even, salty, decadent.

• • •

Old English: *mǣl n.* the time for eating, meal-time, a meal. e.g. *He gereordade æt anum mæle fif þusend manna:* at one meal he fed five thousand men. (Wulfstan)

• • •

I am here for the cicada bruschetta. Being that it is the Brood II year of periodical cicadas, I have seen these sky prawns clinging to magnolia trunks, their metamorphosed bodies in flight, and the possibility of biting into one sends a zingy current through my stomach and palms. It may be my only opportunity to prove myself more courageous than Russell Crowe, who refused to pop a barbequed delicacy into his mouth alongside Jay Leno on *The Tonight Show.*

I also hope to glean new recipes, considering I have a herd of 2,000 mealworms pasturing in a plastic storage bin in Virginia. While I'm away, they receive a daily cabbage leaf from my mother, who has been a farmer's daughter, granddaughter, a farmer, a farmer's wife, and now, a mini-livestock farmer's mother. Their bed of rolled oats simmers at a cold boil, writhing with a constant rain-on-the-roof sound of activity. With their poor eyes buried in a divot of potato, they keep at their voracious munching when light opens on their drawer. Other tan curls slip into that darkness available beneath edible soil.

• • •

Due to their resemblance to the "tequila worm," mealys are often used in tequila-flavored candies. Neither are there worms in the bottom of Jose Cuervo, although an occasional bottle of mezcal does contain the larvae of the moth *Hypopta agavis,* included as a marketing gimmick in the 1940s. Also known as *chinicuiles,* they feed on the *Agave americana* plant but are not considered pests since they are eaten in Mexican dishes, bathed in hot sauce, dandled with green chili and onion, and then swaddled in tortillas.

Though insects have not been widely cultivated for food, the Aztecs of Mesoamerica are thought to have sustained their population-dense society on insects and insect eggs. It is not certain whether they harvested naturally occurring species or domesticated them, but they managed protein sources without large domestic animals.

• • •

My name is on the press list thanks to an invitation from Marcel Dicke, winner of the Dutch Nobel Prize, the NWO-Spinoza Award, and co-author of *The Insect Cookbook.* We have been corresponding via email for months, since I discovered the professor would be a visiting scholar at Cornell University and more accessible for an interview than when at his usual desk at Wageningen University in The Netherlands.

"It's going to happen," Dicke tells me, "I don't expect the change to be over night, but if Coca-Cola were to stop advertising today, their sales would go down. We must repeat this message. In the Netherlands we've repeated it all over."

The message is: "We need to re-examine our relationship to insects."

The message is: "Insects contribute approximately 57 billion dollars a year to society by removing waste, pollinating crops, controlling pests, and serving as a food source for animals higher on the food chain."

The message is: "A healthy vegetarian diet is not always possible for everyone, for various reasons."

The message is: "Eighty percent of the world already eats insects."

The message is: "In terms of biomass, insects are more abundant than we are."

The message is: "Insects are already present in allowable quantities in such foods as canned tomato soup, peanut butter, chocolate."

The message is: "Cochineal insects are used to dye imitation crab meat, red M&M's, pie fillings, sausages, fruit juices, etc."

•   •   •

On the drive to D.C., I pass through the Shenandoah Valley on a June day unseasonably cool enough to have my windows down. A Dragonhunter, or Black Clubtail, darts in and catches a three hundred-mile lift. By far the largest clubtail in North America, the species is named for the males' habit of curling their abdomens underneath them while flying, to form a J shape. Landed, its wings span six inches on the back seat and resemble a pair of hairpin lace panties. Yellow segments stripe a 3.7-inch body. Its bright green, corn-kernel-sized orbs stare back with 30,00 lenses like mine, unblinking.

• • •

Meal *n.* a coarse, unsifted powder ground from the edible part of a grain or pulse ground to powder: wheatmeal; cornmeal, or any ground substance, as of nuts or seeds, resembling this.

• • •

Pat Crowley, one of the first insect entrepreneurs to promote edible insects to American audiences, named his company Chapul after the *Nahuatl* (Aztec) word for cricket. Inspired by Aztec and ancient Puebloan techniques for drying crickets and grasshoppers and milling them into protein-rich breads, Chapul makes high protein energy bars that include cricket powder. One popular variety is the Aztec bar, which uses familiar favorite ingredients like dark chocolate, coffee, and cayenne pepper to re-introduce North Americans to this ancient protein.

• • •

Crickets are efficient converters of grain at almost 1:1 gram produced per gram ingested, requiring twelve times less feed than cattle to produce the same amount of protein, which cultivation could dramatically reduce greenhouse gas emissions.

• • •

Dicke proposes large-scale cultivation of these efficient creatures that can and are being fed on apple juice pulp and other food wastes, are social enough to like crowded conditions, cannot communicate diseases across nervous systems with humans, and, in certain species, contain omega-3 fatty acids in proportion to fish.

Plus, unlike my parents' starter-herd purchase of a Black Angus calf named Mikey, which I bottlefed until weaned, mealys can come of age in my one-bedroom apartment.

• • •

Meal *n.* informal—make a meal of, to perform (a task) with unnecessarily great effort.

·   ·   ·

What sent me over that incredible divide to become an insectivore who dines weekly on six-legged proteins is that there is no butchery involved. Granted, there is death, an entropic tradeoff between one creature and another, but no knives or dressing are required. Perhaps that perk seems hypocritical. I accept that. Growing up surrounded by Whiteface, Midnight, Sukie, Nike, etc. with a freezer full of beef trains one to make discomfiting decisions.

My grandmother, who would swing a chicken by the neck to kill it, died when I was seven. No one kept the hen house operative when she was gone, so it is not pet birds I recall when standing over polythene-wrapped trays of poultry. I learned to cook tofu, blanche almonds, boil beans to add to my salsa—rather than slice through white tendons and trim gristle.

·   ·   ·

Black with hardened front wings, or elytra, darkling beetles are twice as large as ladybugs, which thankfully for farmers are no ladies to aphids. Equally harmless tickling across human hands, darkling beetles have no polka dots to entertain children but will feign death by standing on their heads.

·   ·   ·

The texture and flavor variety in over 1,000 edible insect species has them increasingly available on gourmet menus in London, The Netherlands, and New York, entering the mainstream the way sushi did, ironically, since both food sources have been enjoyed for centuries.

·   ·   ·

At my current micro-herd size, I keep a roughly two-and-a-half-pound supply of mealys in my freezer. If I want to add protein to my tossed salad or crunch to a slice of pineapple-tomato pizza, I pull out a handful and run them under cold water. Two to three minutes in a sauté pan with a splash of oil and a shake of pepper, and they sizzle like steam hissing from a crab's leg.

Bowing my hand over the plate, I examine the gold, amber, brown variation of their bodies. Two weeks ago, they were slimmer than a grain of quinoa, and now they are wide as a spaghetti noodle. Though they grew on their own, I am proud. They depended on me to bring them kale leaves, which they chewed to a thread, apple cores, celery ends, yam skins. They made a living right there in my laundry room, on the wealth of my scraps, oftentimes while I slept.

• • •

The message is: "Grasshoppers have 5 mg. of iron vs. 3.5 in beef."
The message is: "Skewered and roasted with salt and vinegar, you'd be surprised how delicious water boatmen are."
The message is: "Higher consciousness about our nutritional sources is imperative."
The message is: "Look into a locust's eyes. They are beautiful, striated. People ask Dicke, 'How can you look into the eyes of something you are going to eat?' He says, 'How can you not?'"

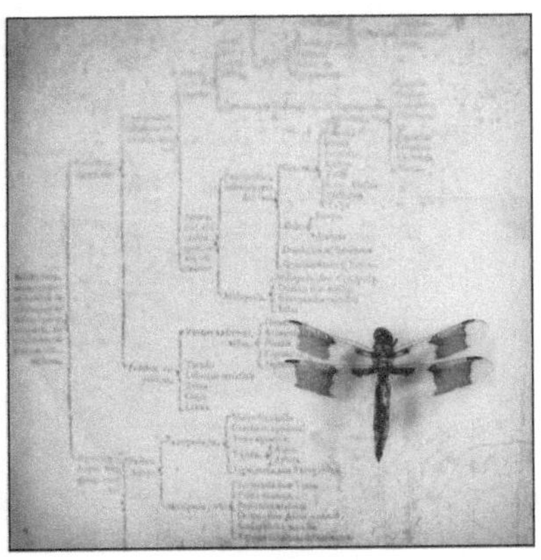

Melu

Melu n. from the Old English for meal, a coarse powder milled from nuts, seeds, or any substance resembling this, not to be confused with *melee,* a struggle, especially a hand-to-hand fight among several people, a fracas—not a *mess,* any number of humans who meal together.

• • •

It was important to my mother that our family ate dinner together, so there were only a few times a year when an away game would prevent my sharing the table with my parents and younger brother. The cheerleading bus would stop at some fast food establishment, and our ravenous claque would slide into laminate booths to gush ketchup onto our fries and white skirts. Too young to miss the company of my family, I did pine for beef from my grandfather's farm, hot off the backyard grill, when I bit into those commercial quarter pounders.

• • •

With college came front doors that opened onto concrete and asphalt rather than rolling fields set aside for cattle. The farm that has been in my family for over six generations grew in significance as an increasing number of small-scale operations were pinched like cookie dough and shipped off in ice cream cartons to someone else's party.

• • •

There are huge panoramic photographs hanging in the Canton, Ohio, airport depicting acres of farmland before and after the building of the airport. The intention seems to be to demonstrate this once rural community's connection to a larger world, but the images stop me mid-route, hurrying through the terminal on my way to a writers' conference. I stand stunned before them while dozens of other travelers rush past. I want them to notice this loss. I want to spend the storm of my fear and fury on some official, and for construction all over the world to stop and begin again with a better plan. But I reason with myself that the damage has already been done and, after all, here I am taking advantage of this resource traded years ago for natural ones.

• • •

Though familiar with grasshoppers bounding over my family's farm, I did not know they are edible and higher in iron than beef. I look across the same pastures after learning it, imagining how many millions of grasshoppers could feed on a single acre, churning out protein at twelve times the efficiency rate of cattle without the high cost of greenhouse gases. With my agrarian heritage in mind, I welcome this opportunity to lighten humanity's environmental footprint.

In addition to helping address the global nutritional demand for humans expected by 2050, the United Nations released a report titled *Edible Insects: Future prospects for food and feed security,* which suggests that the large-scale cultivation of select species of ants, crickets, cicadas, dragonflies, mealworms, etc. could also improve bio-waste management, and produce more ecological livestock feed.

• • •

In their Rubbermaid barn, my mini-livestock herd of mealworms forms an alphabet soup of letters, spelling out an S, I, and an M. They crawl over each other writing. They prophesy in patterns like tea leaves, their fawn tails purling question marks. One lifts its head to form a three-dimensional P. Henry David Thoreau's "Simplify!" can be made out in tawny curls, although the message demands more of contemporary readers, whose lives are not only complicated by railroads but also airplanes, single-car drivers, carbon emissions, groundwater pollution, and over-fished oceans.

Growing up middle-class but surrounded by natural riches, my brother and I both thought of running away at various points in our lives. Before either of us had read *Walden,* we imagined walking into the mountains, knowing the land could support us. Even as logging roads lacing the forests were growing steadily wider and the cleared land was being developed, an aspect of the American Dream was still clinging like limestone salamanders to the Blue Ridge.

Parcels of mountain land were affordable enough for a motorcycle mechanic to move down from Pennsylvania, purchase an eighth of an acre, and build a one-room cabin without running water or electricity. We would pass him on the road sometimes, on foot, and if there was room in the car or back of the truck, Dad would pick him up. This revolutionary pushed the boundaries of civilization as we knew it, and became the figure who, when I did read Thoreau, made such wild decisions seem possible, even inevitable.

I am a proponent of whole foods and frequent the periphery of my local grocery where the lettuces, raw almonds, and fresh coconut milk reside. My friends send periodic emails relaying the health benefits of chia seeds and on social media debate the advantages of cooked vs. uncooked kale. When a new supermarket opens one block from my house with a produce department that stocks aloe leaves, jicama, and pomegranates in January, I thrill at this bounty, wondering what my grandmother would say, who used to can pears and apples from their orchard to perk up a winter plate.

My generation has an advantage over my grandmother's in terms of food quantity, thanks to a far-flung human network, but my mother, a connoisseur of quality foods, points out the degradation of shipped supermarket produce compared to local species. She plucks sweet yellow Lodi apples ripe from the tree and tart Summer Rambos to perfect her pie. Johnson's Red Winters, now thought to be extinct, complement her apple crisp. In addition to featuring less flavor, there is also nutritional degradation in the monoculture supermarket varieties, as there is between store-bought greens and the wild plantain and poke greens that grow in the fields and woods near her house.

In my late twenties, when food choices began to affect the way I feel, I scarfed up information about the importance of whole grain vs. refined flours, trans vs. healthy fat, presuming people who did not make similar decisions were simply unaware of the facts. Gradually, I came to realize the level of processing that so many articles lambasted was not always a result of ignorance, but often an attempt to stretch resources. While I could justify the extra expense of certain brands of tortillas that contained a higher proportion of organically grown grains or kernels, I realized everyone did not have that option. Nor would the industry be able to supply enough corn or wheat if chemical fertilizers were not added to the soil.

The latter realization humbled my purchases, realigned my ideals with reality. We could not provide enough organic corn for humans unless we dramatically rerouted the supply used to bulk up livestock, fatten trout. Those articles I read so diligently did not footnote that our rivers do not in fact contain a wild salmon for every plate when eaten twice a week, as recommended, or taken daily in cold-pressed oil capsules. The seemingly bottomless ocean that stocks all-you-can-eat buffet bowls is subject to risks similar to that sky so full of passenger pigeons a hunting party could fire all afternoon and not drop half. We overestimate our wealth.

And underestimate it. Who imagines Thoreau's outcry against luxury applies to such affordable steak burgers?

•   •   •

In the *Second Book of the Tao*, translator Stephen Mitchell contemplates the most famous dream in history, in which Chinese philosopher Chuang-tzu dreamt he was a butterfly, only to wake no longer sure who was the dreamer and which the dream. "How can we know what depths of joy lie hidden within that pinpoint of a brain?" Mitchell asks those less able to interchange points of view with a butterfly. I think of his question while watching my mealworm larvae. Do they have an inkling of the transformation that awaits them? And if they do dream of the darkling beetles they will become, are they not preparing them by filling their crops with the most oats and other foodstuffs available? Complete metamorphosis being the follow-through of their lives, the last stop on the train they boarded at birth, they are not trying to pack light.

•   •   •

Thanks to socio-economic progress, the numbers of hungry or undernourished people have decreased nearly thirty percent in Asia and the Pacific in the last three years. Latin America and the Caribbean also made strides, falling from sixty-five million hungry in the early nineties to forty-nine million by 2010. These numbers are encouraging but tempered by a rise of hunger in developed regions, which increased by three million from 2006 to 2012, reversing a steady decrease in previous years. Redistribution is happening, the Food and Agriculture Organization says, but the numbers remain unacceptable, with one in eight people living globally with inadequate nourishment.

•   •   •

While I write this sentence, the World Population Clock clicks from 7,119,381,578 to 7,119,381,749.

•   •   •

The most severe extinction event ever known occurred during the Permian-Triassic period two hundred fifty-two million years ago. More catastrophic than the Cretaceous-Tertiary Extinction sixty-five million years ago that wiped out the dinosaurs, the "Great Dying" is the only known mass extinction of insects, making prior fossil records for ancient species like darkling beetles that originated 300 million or more years ago rare finds. I compare their time line with arrowheads my grandfather would unearth on the farm, evidence of another world that then seemed so long ago.

•   •   •

The demand for meat is rising disproportionate to the population, because it is not merely the number of humans on the rise but also the corresponding amount of meat they are consuming. The largest current demand comes from the United States, with 265 lbs. averaged per person annually. Europe follows at 166 lbs. The level is also rising in the developing nations whose low 20 lb. consumption has more than doubled to 44 lbs. in recent years, as they follow the unsustainable model of developed nations.

In an attempt to answer the expected 73 percent increase in the demand for meat, Dutch biologist Mark Post is culturing cattle stem cells in petri dishes. Post says they grow the tissue in a doughnut-shaped ring, with cells placed around a mound of "nutrient gel."

•　•　•

Mileu n. the physical or social setting in which people live or in which something happens or develops. Origin French from *mi* + *lieu.*

•　•　•

The plastic mealy bin opens like a room that has been enclosed with sleep, though they do not sleep. Lights on or off, dusk or two a.m., the mini-barn aerates like shore sand. Their all-consuming appetites drive them to stock their bodies with energy stores. Later will be breeding time, after they have adequately fueled their bodies for change. Writhing in their plastic drawers like a boxful of kittens, they make pleasant company. In their furor for living they spill over my fingers like dry beans, cling to my thumb like Lilliputian gymnasts.

When friends wonder at my adoration of creatures I plan to ingest, I find it crueler to imagine the inverse. Living among and tending animals makes me full of gratitude and acknowledgment for the interdependence of life.

•　•　•

August 5, 2013, taste-testers in London declare the $330,000 lab-grown hamburger's flavor to be "close to meat." An Austrian food researcher notes it is "not that juicy" compared to standard burgers, but Chicago-based journalist Josh Schonwald reasons its dryness is due to a lower fat content than traditional beef.

Scientist-turned-chef, Post explains that bread crumb binders, salt, and egg powder supplement the textural consistency or "mouth appeal," while saffron and beet juice augment color. Currently the product is too expensive for commercial purposes, but many anticipate technology will soon advance to make mass-marketing possible. *Atlantic Monthly* writer Alexis Madrigal compiles a chart of predictions that beef—as well as lab-grown sausage, poultry, and lamb—could be commercially available with current funding anywhere from 2020 to 2035.

•　•　•

I imagine a ground mealworm patty might be packed with oats and grilled like a burger, but I grind some into cornbread instead—because a local farmer gave me a bag of Cherokee corn.

•　•　•

Ela or *elo n*. Cherokee word for earth.

•　•　•

Though more common images of Native Americans portray hunters mounted on horseback and roaming the plains in search of buffalo, there were many agrarian Village Indians who developed bottomlands into garden plots. Tribes like the Cheyenne, Dakota, and Comanche were favored in Westerns and history books, while few romanticized the Hidatsa, Mandan, and Arikara for their complex agricultural legacies. Yet these tribes sustained themselves on the same land year after year by developing sustainable practices, recorded in a rare anthropological preservation of a woman's account of tribal life in the mid 1800s, *Buffalo Bird Woman's Garden: Agriculture of the Hidatsa Indians*.

• • •

The blue and white ears I grind are from a sacred heirloom seed called White Eagle, entrusted by a Cherokee descendant to my partner Don, an organic farmer. After harvest, he sets aside a bag for the local tribe as he does every year, and this season offered a few ears to me.

Lacking a recipe for blue cornbread, I turn to *Buffalo Bird Woman's Garden* as well as to several cookbooks, including *American Indian Cooking and Herb Lore,* which has a recipe for the delicacy, Yellow-Jacket Soup.

Though traditional Cherokee ground corn under mortar and pestle, coffee grinders are more often used today. I pulp the hard kernels plucked from the cobs with a turbo blender. "It doesn't get any more whole grain than this," I tell my mother, calling to ask if she uses flour in her recipe since several suggest a mix. I want this bread to crumble moist into a bowl of beans the way her corn muffins do.

• • •

Selu n. the Cherokee word for corn, named for the Corn-mother, or First Woman, the spirit who protects the harvest.

• • •

When Andrew Jackson's Indian Removal Act forced the relocation of more than 16,000 Cherokee during the severe winter of 1838-1839, the nation had to squeeze onto smaller territories of land. One of the provisions the ousted Cherokee brought with them during the Trail of Tears was White Eagle corn. Named for the white vein that appears on certain blue kernels, this breed is streaked with what appears to be outstretched wings of an eagle in flight.

Studying the figure on a number of the kernels I was given, I imagine that totem's comfort accompanying their move. How gemlike these kernels would become in the face of 4,000 deaths due to illness and hunger. I turn the talon-scratched sapphires in the light and they starburst like moonstones.

• • •

The mealy bin corners teem with small pyramids of bronze entwined bodies that, unlike cattle, pigs, chickens, and some humans, thrive in crowded conditions. Though their bin is large enough for each to sequester himself in sheets of oats, they toss their bedding and band together, plaited into miniature ropes.

They scale kale leaves like Frost's swingers of birches, jungle-gym collard spines. A working circus, they spin oats into protein at approximately one gram per gram ingested, as opposed to the eight or nine grams lost by cattle, unwieldy performers whose hooves can't reach the same whirling pedals.

Compared to 16-19 g. in tilapia, and 13-27 in shrimp, mealworms contain 14-25 g. of protein (per 100 g.). Also, their omega-3 fatty acid proportions are similar to fish, while their iron, copper, zinc, selenium, and potassium content correspond to beef.

• • •

For the first batch, I leave the measured cup of frozen and rinsed mealys whole, since unlike bananas, oranges, crustaceans, etc., they may be eaten entire. The second batch I grind in the blender like the corn kernels. While their bodies jut like raisins from the first loaves, the ground batch is the clear winner.

After the iron skillet cools, I flip the pan and pop a crusty loaf onto a wire rack. Blue corn kernels fleck the bread like blueberry fragments. These thick slices have a natural grain sweetness that disguises any evidence the meal is enriched with ento-protein, vitamin B12, and essential linoleic acids, except that it satiates my appetite longer than plain cornbread.

• • •

The World Population Clock now reads 7,120,067,908... 7,120,067,921... 7,120,067,933....

· · ·

Mealys rarely pause, but when one does, it rests full length against a slice of potato the way a fevered child might press a cheek to a cool tile floor. It nuzzles into a lettuce hammock like a father napping after mowing the lawn. Trooping ever forward, coated with oat dust, they slip flour-faced and frictionless between trap doors in the grain. One clings to my finger when I lift the bin to sift out frass, allowing me to honor Thoreau's *Walden* invective to "keep your accounts on your thumb-nail." It noses me in curiosity while I envision mess halls all over the world growing pacific as diners clink their mugs over loaves of golden bread.

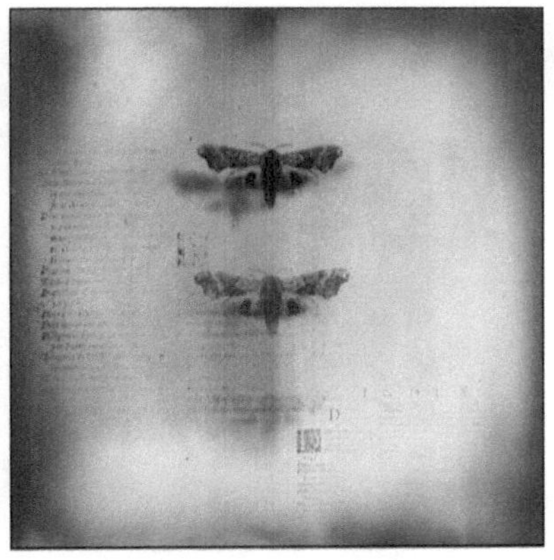

For Further Reading

"Allergy Statistics." American Academy of Allergy, Asthma and Immunology, www.aaaai.org.

Cabral, Javier. "Eat Your Crickets: Los Angeles Is the Chapuline Capitol of the U.S." *Los Angeles Times*, www.latimes.com.

Chrusciel, Ewa. 2014. *Contraband of Hoopoe*. Omnidawn.

Collis, John Stewart. 1954. *The Triumph of the Tree*. Sloane Press Archive.

Dicke, Marcel. 2010. "Why Not Eat Insects?" TedTalk.

Elardi, Frank. "There's a Cricket in My Energy Bar." *ABC News*, www.abcnews.go.com.

Frost, S.W. 1959. *Insect Life and Insect Natural History*. Dover Publications.

Goldstein, Paul. "Modern Physics and the Shamir." Kabbalah Online, www.chabad.org.

Hayden, Brian. 1992. "Models of Domestication." Anne Birgitte Gebauer and T. Douglas Price. *Transitions to Agriculture in Prehistory*. Prehistory Press.

Hole, Frank. "A Reassessment of the Neolithic Revolution." *Paléorient*: 10.2, 1984.

"Household Food Security in the United States." U.S. Department of Agriculture Economic Research Service, www.ers.usda.gov.

Huis, Arnold van, et. al. "Edible Insects: Future Prospects for Food and Feed Security." Food and Agricultural Organization of the United Nations, 2013.

Kunstmann, John Gotthold. 2014. *The Hoopoe: A Study in European Folklore*. A reprinted 1938 dissertation. Nabu Press.

Lesnik, Julie. 2018. *Edible Insects and Human Evolution*. University of Florida Press.

Madrigal, Alexis. "Chart: When Will We Eat Hamburgers Grown in Test Tubes?" *Atlantic Monthly*, www.theatlantic.com.

Milosz, Czeslaw. 2001. "Into the Tree." *New and Collected Poems*. The Ecco Press.

Mitchell, Stephen, ed. 2009. *The Second Book of the Tao*. Penguin.

"Scientists to cook world's first in-vitro beef burger." Reuters, www.reuters.com.

Robinson, Jo. "Breeding the Nutrition Out of Our Food." *The New York Times*, www.nytimes.com.

Shulman, Martha Rose. "Just Don't Call Them Weeds." *The New York Times*, www.nytimes.com.

Siemianowska, Ewa, et. al. "Larvae of mealworm (*Tenebrio molitor* L.) as European novel food." *Agricultural Sciences*, Vol. 4., No. 6, 2013.

Smith, Michael. 2002. *The Aztecs*. Wiley Blackwell.

"The State of Food Insecurity in the World." Food and Agriculture Organization, www.fao.org/state-of-food-security-nutrition

Tonino, Leath. "The Egret Lifting from the River: David Hinton on the Wisdom of Ancient Chinese Poets." *The Sun*, January, Issue 469, 2015.

"Top Fifteen Agricultural Exporters and Importers." World Trade Organization, www.wto.org.

Underwood, Thomas. 1973. *American Indian Cooking and Herb Lore*. Cherokee Publications.

"World Population Clock." United States Census Bureau. www.census.gov/popclock.

van der Veen, Marijke. "Agricultural Innovation: Invention and Adoption or Change and Adaptation?" *World Archeology*, 42.1, 1989.

Weiner, Miriam. "Countries that Eat Bugs." *U.S. News & World Report*, 28 April 2011.

Wilson, Gilbert. 1987. *Buffalo Bird Woman's Garden: Agriculture of the Hidatsa Indians*. Minnesota Historical Society Press.

"World Hunger and Poverty Facts and Statistics." World Hunger Education Service, www.worldhunger.org

Amy Wright is the author of two poetry books, one collaboration, and six chapbooks. Most recently her essays won first place in two contests, sponsored by *London Magazine* and *Quarterly West*. She has also received two Peter Taylor Fellowships to the *Kenyon Review* Writer's Workshop, an Individual Artist Grant from the Tennessee Arts Commission, and a fellowship to Virginia Center for the Creative Arts. Her essays appear in *Brevity, Fourth Genre, Georgia Review, Ninth Letter, Waveform: Anthology of Women Essayists,* and elsewhere.